ENSEMBLE DEVELOPMENT

Chorales and Warm-up Exercises for Tone, Technique and Rhythm

INTERMEDIATE CONCERT BAND

Peter **BOONSHAFT** | Chris **BERNOTAS**

Thank you for making *Sound Innovations: Ensemble Development* a part of your concert band curriculum. With 412 exercises, including over 70 chorales by some of today's most renowned composers for concert band, it is our hope you will find this book to be a valuable resource in helping you grow in your understanding and abilities as an ensemble musician.

An assortment of exercises are grouped by key and presented in a variety of intermediate difficulty levels. Where possible, several exercises in the same category are provided to allow for variety while accomplishing the goals of that specific type of exercise. You will notice that many exercises and chorales are clearly marked with dynamics, articulations, style, and tempo for you to practice those aspects of performance. Other exercises are intentionally left for you or your teacher to determine how best to use them in reaching your performance goals.

Whether you are progressing through exercises to better your technical facility or to challenge your musicianship with beautiful chorales, we are confident you will be excited, motivated, and inspired by using *Sound Innovations: Ensemble Development*.

© 2012 Alfred Music Publishing Co., Inc.
Sound Innovations™ is a trademark of Alfred Music Publishing Co., Inc.
All Rights Reserved including Public Performance

ISBN-10: 0-7390-6772-9
ISBN-13: 978-0-7390-6772-7

Instrument photos courtesy of Yamaha Corporation of America Band & Orchestral Division

Concert B♭ Major (Your C Major)

1   **PASSING THE TONIC**

2   **PASSING THE TONIC**

3   **PASSING THE TONIC**

4   **PASSING THE TONIC**

5   **PASSING THE TONIC**

6   **BREATHING AND LONG TONES**

7   **BREATHING AND LONG TONES**

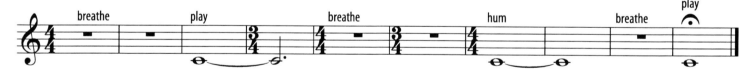

8   **BREATHING AND LONG TONES**

9   **BREATHING AND LONG TONES**

3

CONCERT B♭ MAJOR SCALE (YOUR C MAJOR SCALE)

SCALE PATTERN

SCALE PATTERN

SCALE PATTERN

SCALE PATTERN

SCALE PATTERN

CHANGING SCALE RHYTHM

CONCERT B♭ CHROMATIC SCALE (YOUR C CHROMATIC SCALE)

4

18 FLEXIBILITY

19 FLEXIBILITY

20 ARPEGGIOS

21 ARPEGGIOS

22 INTERVALS

23 INTERVALS

24 BALANCE AND INTONATION: PERFECT INTERVALS

25 BALANCE AND INTONATION: DIATONIC HARMONY

26 BALANCE AND INTONATION: FAMILY BALANCE

BALANCE AND INTONATION: LAYERED TUNING

BALANCE AND INTONATION: MOVING CHORD TONES

BALANCE AND INTONATION: SHIFTING CHORD QUALITIES

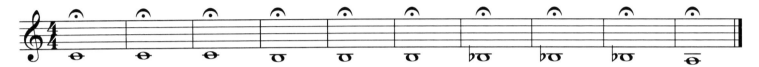

EXPANDING INTERVALS: DOWNWARD IN PARALLEL OCTAVES

EXPANDING INTERVALS: DOWNWARD IN PARALLEL FIFTHS

EXPANDING INTERVALS: DOWNWARD IN TRIADS

EXPANDING INTERVALS: UPWARD IN PARALLEL OCTAVES

EXPANDING INTERVALS: UPWARD IN TRIADS

RHYTHM

36 **RHYTHM**

37 **RHYTHM**

38 **RHYTHM**

39 **RHYTHM**

40 **RHYTHMIC SUBDIVISION**

41 **RHYTHMIC SUBDIVISION**

42 **RHYTHMIC SUBDIVISION**

43 **METER**

7

PHRASING

PHRASING

ARTICULATION

DYNAMICS

ETUDE

Moderately

ETUDE

Stately

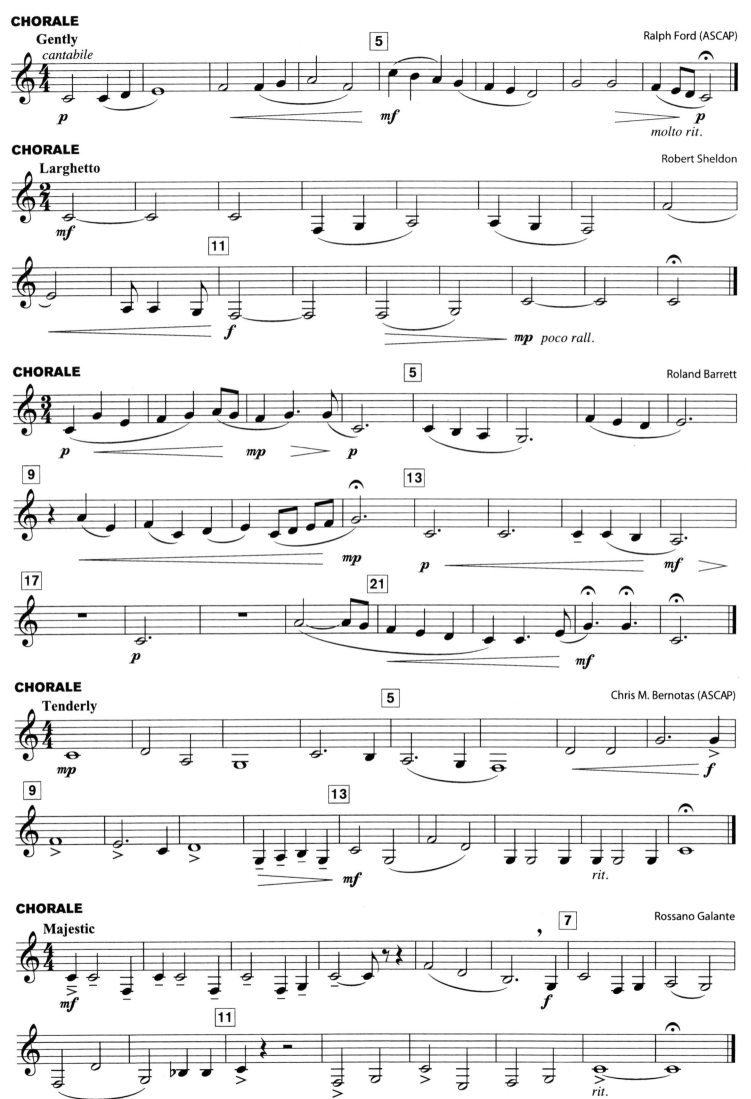

Concert G Minor (Your A Minor)

61 PASSING THE TONIC

62 BREATHING AND LONG TONES

63 CONCERT G NATURAL MINOR SCALE (YOUR A NATURAL MINOR SCALE)

64 CONCERT G HARMONIC AND MELODIC MINOR SCALES

65 SCALE PATTERN

66 CONCERT G CHROMATIC SCALE (YOUR A CHROMATIC SCALE)

67 FLEXIBILITY

68 FLEXIBILITY

69 ARPEGGIOS

ARPEGGIOS

INTERVALS

INTERVALS

BALANCE AND INTONATION: DIATONIC HARMONY

BALANCE AND INTONATION: MOVING CHORD TONES

BALANCE AND INTONATION: LAYERED TUNING

BALANCE AND INTONATION: FAMILY BALANCE

EXPANDING INTERVALS: DOWNWARD IN PARALLEL FIFTHS

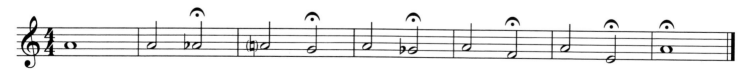

EXPANDING INTERVALS: UPWARD IN PARALLEL THIRDS

12

79 RHYTHM

80 RHYTHM

81 RHYTHM

82 RHYTHMIC SUBDIVISION

83 RHYTHMIC SUBDIVISION

84 ARTICULATION AND DYNAMICS

85 ETUDE

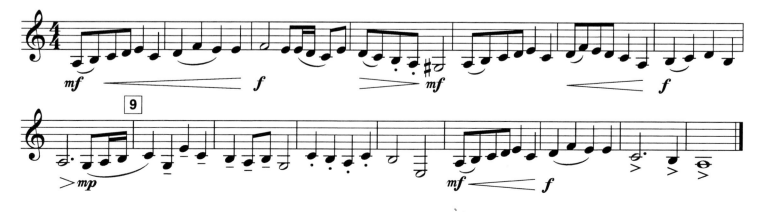

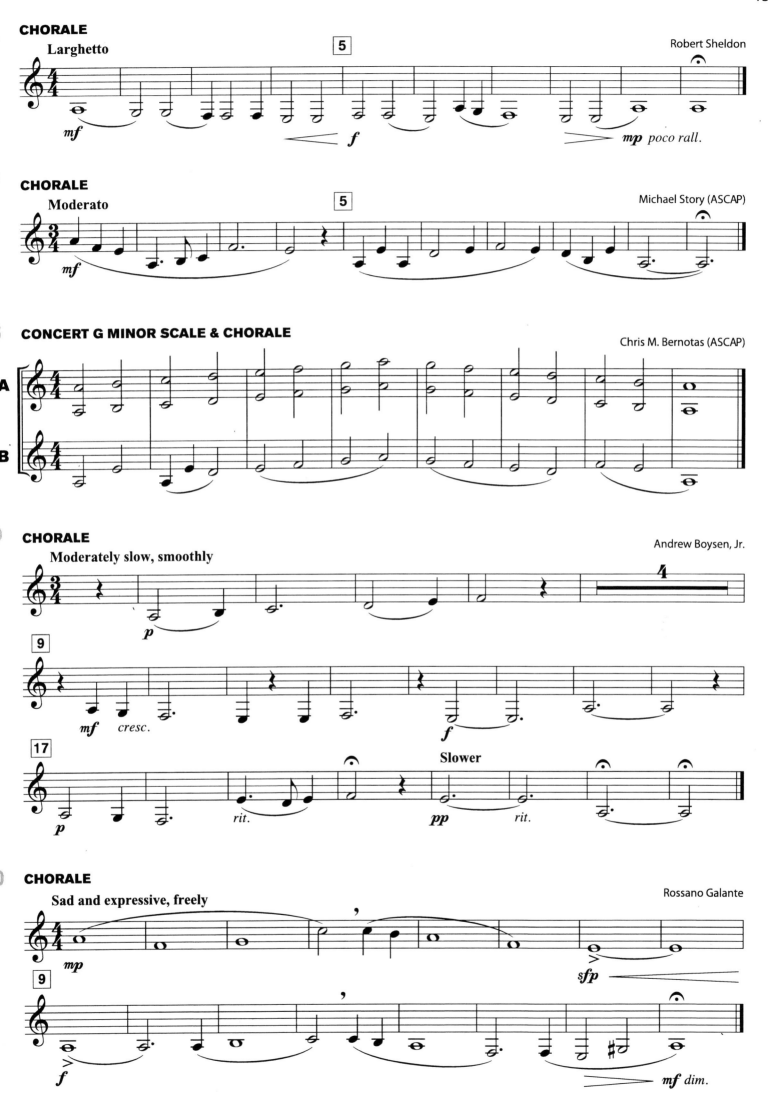

Concert E♭ Major (Your F Major)

91   PASSING THE TONIC

92   PASSING THE TONIC

93   PASSING THE TONIC

94   PASSING THE TONIC

95   PASSING THE TONIC

96   BREATHING AND LONG TONES

97   BREATHING AND LONG TONES

98   BREATHING AND LONG TONES

99   BREATHING AND LONG TONES

CONCERT E♭ MAJOR SCALE (YOUR F MAJOR SCALE)

SCALE PATTERN

SCALE PATTERN

SCALE PATTERN

SCALE PATTERN

SCALE PATTERN

CHANGING SCALE RHYTHM

CONCERT E♭ CHROMATIC SCALE (YOUR F CHROMATIC SCALE)

16

108 FLEXIBILITY

109 FLEXIBILITY

110 ARPEGGIOS

111 ARPEGGIOS

112 INTERVALS

113 INTERVALS

114 BALANCE AND INTONATION: PERFECT INTERVALS

115 BALANCE AND INTONATION: DIATONIC HARMONY

116 BALANCE AND INTONATION: FAMILY BALANCE

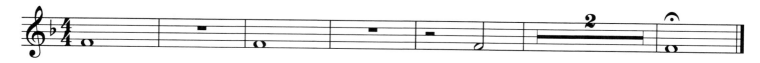

17 BALANCE AND INTONATION: LAYERED TUNING

18 BALANCE AND INTONATION: LAYERED TUNING

19 BALANCE AND INTONATION: SHIFTING CHORD QUALITIES

20 EXPANDING INTERVALS: DOWNWARD IN PARALLEL OCTAVES

21 EXPANDING INTERVALS: DOWNWARD IN PARALLEL FIFTHS

22 EXPANDING INTERVALS: DOWNWARD IN TRIADS

23 EXPANDING INTERVALS: UPWARD IN PARALLEL OCTAVES

24 EXPANDING INTERVALS: UPWARD IN TRIADS

125 **RHYTHM**

126 **RHYTHM**

127 **RHYTHM**

128 **RHYTHM**

129 **RHYTHM**

130 **RHYTHMIC SUBDIVISION**

131 **RHYTHMIC SUBDIVISION**

132 **RHYTHMIC SUBDIVISION**

METER

PHRASING

PHRASING

ARTICULATION

DYNAMICS

ETUDE

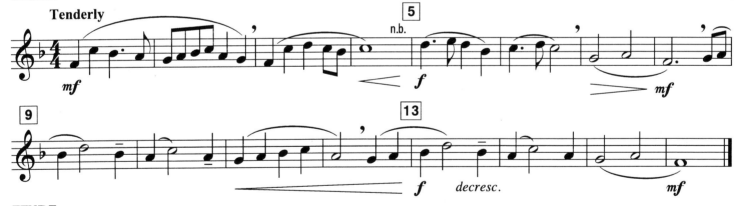

ETUDE

140 **CHORALE**

Adagio, wistfully

Todd Stalter

141 **CHORALE**

Randall D. Standridge (ASCAP)

142 **CONCERT E♭ MAJOR SCALE & CHORALE**

Chris M. Bernotas (ASCAP)

143 **CHORALE**

Moderato

Michael Story (ASCAP)

144 **CHORALE**

Slow and delicate

Andrew Boysen, Jr.

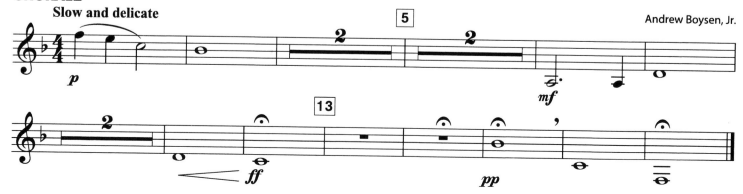

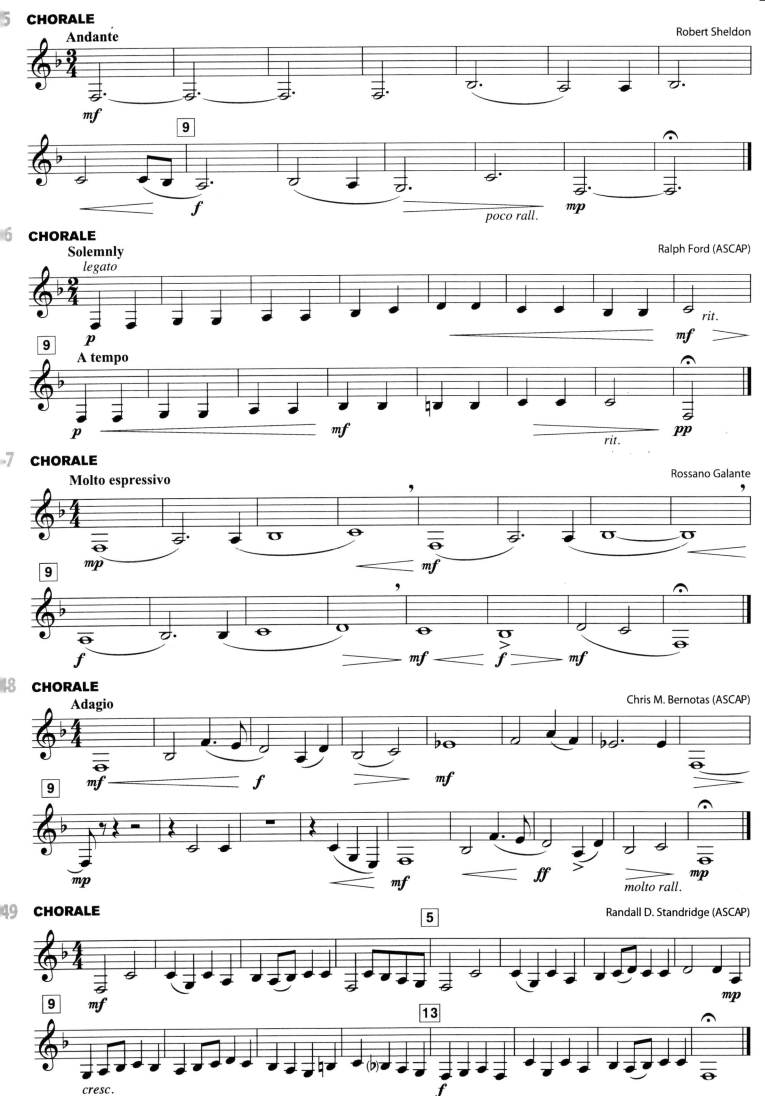

Concert C Minor (Your D Minor)

150 PASSING THE TONIC

151 BREATHING AND LONG TONES

152 CONCERT C NATURAL MINOR SCALE (YOUR D NATURAL MINOR SCALE)

153 CONCERT C HARMONIC AND MELODIC MINOR SCALES

154 SCALE PATTERN

155 CONCERT C CHROMATIC SCALE (YOUR D CHROMATIC SCALE)

156 FLEXIBILITY

157 FLEXIBILITY

ARPEGGIOS

ARPEGGIOS

INTERVALS

INTERVALS

BALANCE AND INTONATION: DIATONIC HARMONY

BALANCE AND INTONATION: MOVING CHORD TONES

BALANCE AND INTONATION: LAYERED TUNING

BALANCE AND INTONATION: FAMILY BALANCE

EXPANDING INTERVALS: DOWNWARD IN TRIADS

EXPANDING INTERVALS: UPWARD IN TRIADS

168 **RHYTHM**

169 **RHYTHM**

170 **RHYTHM**

171 **RHYTHMIC SUBDIVISION**

172 **RHYTHMIC SUBDIVISION**

173 **ARTICULATION AND DYNAMICS**

174 **ETUDE**

Concert F Major (Your G Major)

180 PASSING THE TONIC

181 BREATHING AND LONG TONES

182 CONCERT F MAJOR SCALE (YOUR G MAJOR SCALE)

183 SCALE PATTERN

184 SCALE PATTERN

185 CONCERT F CHROMATIC SCALE (YOUR G CHROMATIC SCALE)

186 FLEXIBILITY

187 FLEXIBILITY

ARPEGGIOS

ARPEGGIOS

INTERVALS

BALANCE AND INTONATION: DIATONIC HARMONY

BALANCE AND INTONATION: FAMILY BALANCE

BALANCE AND INTONATION: LAYERED TUNING

BALANCE AND INTONATION: MOVING CHORD TONES

BALANCE AND INTONATION: SHIFTING CHORD QUALITIES

EXPANDING INTERVALS: DOWNWARD IN PARALLEL FIFTHS

EXPANDING INTERVALS: UPWARD IN PARALLEL FIFTHS

198 RHYTHM

199 RHYTHM

200 RHYTHM

201 RHYTHMIC SUBDIVISION

202 RHYTHMIC SUBDIVISION

203 ARTICULATION AND DYNAMICS

204 ETUDE

Moderately

Concert D Minor (Your E Minor)

210 PASSING THE TONIC

211 BREATHING AND LONG TONES

212 CONCERT D NATURAL MINOR SCALE (YOUR E NATURAL MINOR SCALE)

213 CONCERT D HARMONIC AND MELODIC MINOR SCALES

214 SCALE PATTERN

215 SCALE PATTERN

216 CONCERT D CHROMATIC SCALE (YOUR E CHROMATIC SCALE)

217 FLEXIBILITY

18 FLEXIBILITY

19 ARPEGGIOS

20 ARPEGGIOS

21 INTERVALS

22 BALANCE AND INTONATION: DIATONIC HARMONY

23 BALANCE AND INTONATION: FAMILY BALANCE

24 BALANCE AND INTONATION: LAYERED TUNING

25 BALANCE AND INTONATON: MOVING CHORD TONES

26 EXPANDING INTERVALS: DOWNWARD IN TRIADS

27 EXPANDING INTERVALS: UPWARD IN TRIADS

228 RHYTHM

229 RHYTHM

230 RHYTHM

231 RHYTHMIC SUBDIVISION

232 RHYTHMIC SUBDIVISION

233 ARTICULATION AND DYNAMICS

234 ETUDE

Lyrical

35 CHORALE

Roland Barrett

36 CHORALE

Slow and grave

Andrew Boysen, Jr.

37 CONCERT D MINOR SCALE & CHORALE

Chris M. Bernotas (ASCAP)

38 CHORALE

Andante

Robert Sheldon

39 CHORALE: PSALM 33

From the Genevan Psalter
Harmonized by Claude Goudimel (c. 1520–1572)
Arranged/Edited by Todd Stalter

Grave

Concert A♭ Major (Your B♭ Major)

240 PASSING THE TONIC

241 BREATHING AND LONG TONES

242 CONCERT A♭ MAJOR SCALE (YOUR B♭ MAJOR SCALE)

243 SCALE PATTERN

244 SCALE PATTERN

245 CONCERT A♭ CHROMATIC SCALE (YOUR B♭ CHROMATIC SCALE)

246 FLEXIBILITY

247 FLEXIBILITY

48 ARPEGGIOS

49 ARPEGGIOS

50 INTERVALS

51 BALANCE AND INTONATION: DIATONIC HARMONY

52 BALANCE AND INTONATION: FAMILY BALANCE

53 BALANCE AND INTONATION: LAYERED TUNING

54 BALANCE AND INTONATION: MOVING CHORD TONES

55 EXPANDING INTERVALS: DOWNWARD IN PARALLEL FIFTHS

56 EXPANDING INTERVALS: UPWARD IN PARALLEL THIRDS

65 CHORALE

Randall D. Standridge (ASCAP)

66 CHORALE

Andrew Boysen, Jr.

67 CONCERT A♭ MAJOR SCALE & CHORALE

Chris M. Bernotas (ASCAP)

68 CHORALE

Ralph Ford (ASCAP)

69 CHORALE

Roland Barrett

Concert F Minor (Your G Minor)

270 PASSING THE TONIC

271 BREATHING AND LONG TONES

272 CONCERT F NATURAL MINOR SCALE (YOUR G NATURAL MINOR SCALE)

273 CONCERT F HARMONIC AND MELODIC MINOR SCALES

274 SCALE PATTERN

275 CONCERT F CHROMATIC SCALE (YOUR G CHROMATIC SCALE)

276 FLEXIBILITY

277 FLEXIBILITY

278 ARPEGGIOS

79 ARPEGGIOS

80 INTERVALS

81 INTERVALS

82 BALANCE AND INTONATION: DIATONIC HARMONY

83 BALANCE AND INTONATION: FAMILY BALANCE

84 BALANCE AND INTONATION: LAYERED TUNING

85 BALANCE AND INTONATION: MOVING CHORD TONES

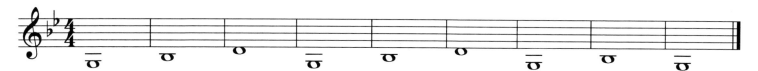

86 EXPANDING INTERVALS: DOWNWARD IN TRIADS

87 EXPANDING INTERVALS: UPWARD IN TRIADS

288 RHYTHM

289 RHYTHM

290 RHYTHM

291 RHYTHMIC SUBDIVISION

292 RHYTHMIC SUBDIVISION

293 ARTICULATION AND DYNAMICS

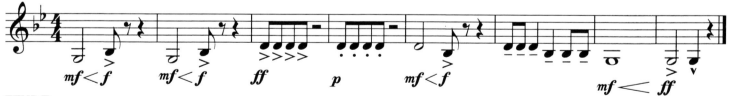

294 ETUDE

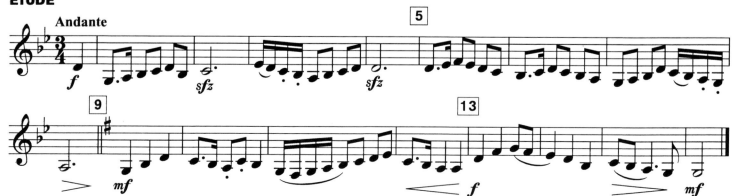

42

Concert D♭ Major (Your E♭ Major)

300 BREATHING AND LONG TONES

301 CONCERT D♭ MAJOR SCALE (YOUR E♭ MAJOR SCALE)

302 SCALE PATTERN

303 SCALE PATTERN

304 SCALE PATTERN

305 FLEXIBILITY

306 ARPEGGIOS

307 INTERVALS

108   BALANCE AND INTONATION: FAMILY BALANCE

109   BALANCE AND INTONATION: LAYERED TUNING

110   EXPANDING INTERVALS: DOWNWARD AND UPWARD IN PARALLEL OCTAVES

111   ARTICULATION AND DYNAMICS

112   ETUDE

Andante

113   ETUDE

Maestoso

114   CHORALE

Moderate, smooth

Andrew Boysen, Jr.

115   CHORALE

Andante religioso

Todd Stalter

Concert B♭ Minor (Your C Minor)

316 BREATHING AND LONG TONES

317 CONCERT B♭ NATURAL MINOR SCALE (YOUR C NATURAL MINOR SCALE)

318 CONCERT B♭ HARMONIC AND MELODIC MINOR SCALES

319 SCALE PATTERN

320 SCALE PATTERN

321 FLEXIBILITY

322 ARPEGGIOS

323 INTERVALS

324 BALANCE AND INTONATION: LAYERED TUNING

25 BALANCE AND INTONATION: MOVING CHORD TONES

26 EXPANDING INTERVALS: DOWNWARD IN TRIADS

27 ARTICULATION AND DYNAMICS

28 ETUDE

Slowly

29 ETUDE

Dramatically

30 CHORALE

Moderately slow

Michael Story (ASCAP)

31 CHORALE

Andante

Robert Sheldon

Concert C Major (Your D Major)

332 BREATHING AND LONG TONES

333 CONCERT C MAJOR SCALE (YOUR D MAJOR SCALE)

334 SCALE PATTERN

335 SCALE PATTERN

336 FLEXIBILITY

337 ARPEGGIOS

338 INTERVALS

339 INTERVALS

340 BALANCE AND INTONATION: FAMILY BALANCE

41 BALANCE AND INTONATION: LAYERED TUNING

42 EXPANDING INTERVALS: DOWNWARD IN PARALLEL FIFTHS

43 ARTICULATION AND DYNAMICS

44 ETUDE

Stately

45 ETUDE

46 CHORALE

Flowingly
molto legato

Ralph Ford (ASCAP)

47 CHORALE: LARGO FROM THE "NEW WORLD SYMPHONY"

Antonín Dvořák
Arranged by Michael Story (ASCAP)

Andante
legato

Concert A Minor (Your B Minor)

348 BREATHING AND LONG TONES

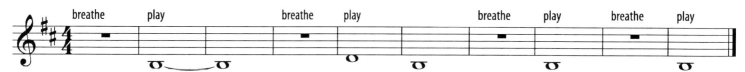

349 CONCERT A NATURAL MINOR SCALE (YOUR B NATURAL MINOR SCALE)

350 CONCERT A HARMONIC AND MELODIC MINOR SCALES

351 SCALE PATTERN

352 FLEXIBILITY

353 ARPEGGIOS

354 INTERVALS

355 INTERVALS

356 BALANCE AND INTONATION: DIATONIC HARMONY

57 **BALANCE AND INTONATION: FAMILY BALANCE**

58 **EXPANDING INTERVALS: DOWNWARD IN TRIADS**

59 **ARTICULATION AND DYNAMICS**

60 **ETUDE**

Slowly, with feeling

61 **ETUDE**

Moderately

62 **CHORALE**

Adagio   Todd Stalter

63 **CHORALE**

Roland Barrett

50

Concert G Major (Your A Major)

364 CONCERT G MAJOR SCALE (YOUR A MAJOR SCALE)

365 BALANCE AND INTONATION: FAMILY BALANCE

366 ETUDE

367 CHORALE

Michael Story (ASCAP)

Concert E Minor (Your F# Minor)

368 CONCERT E NATURAL MINOR SCALE (YOUR F# NATURAL MINOR SCALE)

369 CONCERT E HARMONIC AND MELODIC MINOR SCALES

370 BALANCE AND INTONATION: LAYERED TUNING

371 ETUDE

372 CHORALE

Chris M. Bernotas (ASCAP)

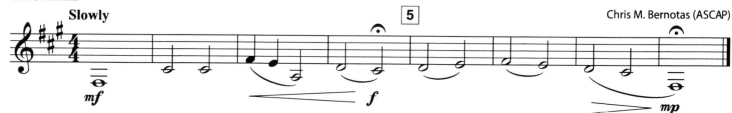

Advancing Rhythm and Meter

383 $\frac{6}{8}$ **METER**

384 $\frac{6}{8}$ **METER**

385 $\frac{6}{8}$ **METER**

386 $\frac{6}{8}$ **METER**

387 $\frac{6}{8}$ **METER**

388 $\frac{6}{8}$ **METER**

389 $\frac{6}{8}$ **METER**

390 $\frac{6}{8}$ **METER**

391 **CHANGING METERS:** $\frac{4}{4}$ **AND** $\frac{6}{8}$

392 **CHANGING METERS:** $\frac{3}{4}$ **AND** $\frac{6}{8}$

93 **TRIPLETS**

94 **TRIPLETS**

95 **TRIPLETS**

96 **TRIPLETS**

97 **TRIPLETS**

98 **TRIPLETS**

99 **TRIPLETS**

100 **TRIPLETS**

101 **TRIPLETS**

102 **TRIPLETS**

403 **3/8 METER**

404 **3/8 METER**

405 **9/8 METER**

406 **9/8 METER**

407 **12/8 METER**

408 **12/8 METER**

409 **5/8 METER**

(2+3)   (3+2)

410 **5/8 METER**

(2+3)   (3+2)

411 **7/8 METER**

(2+2+3)

412 **7/8 METER**

(2+2+3)

Bass Clarinet Fingering Chart

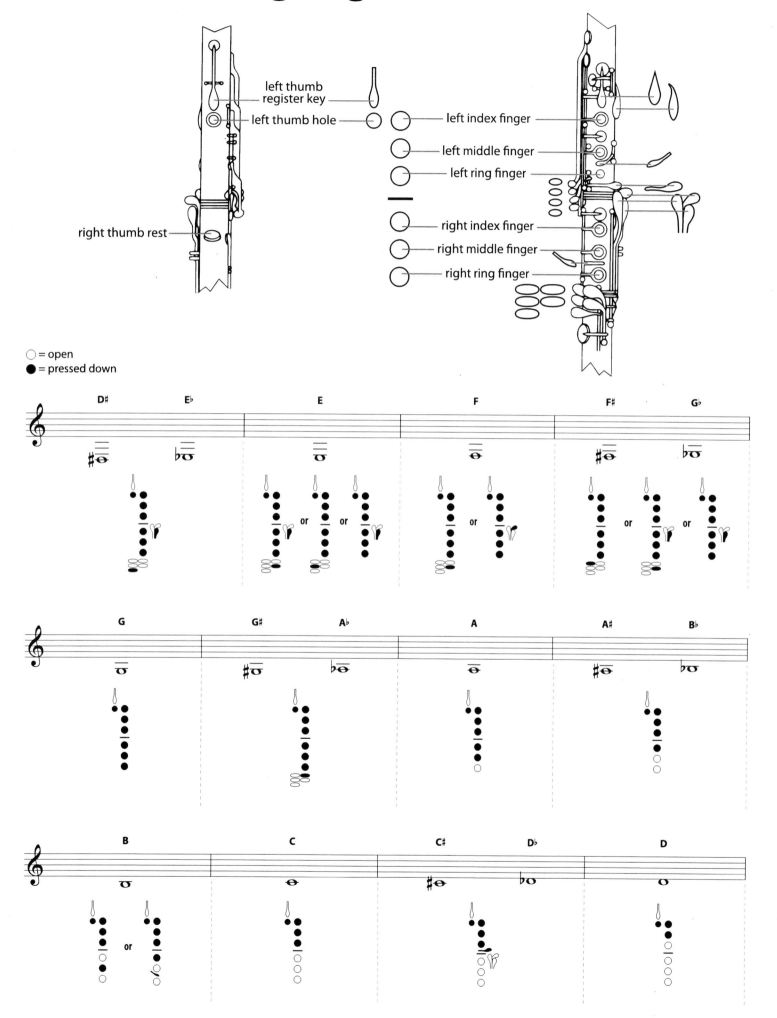

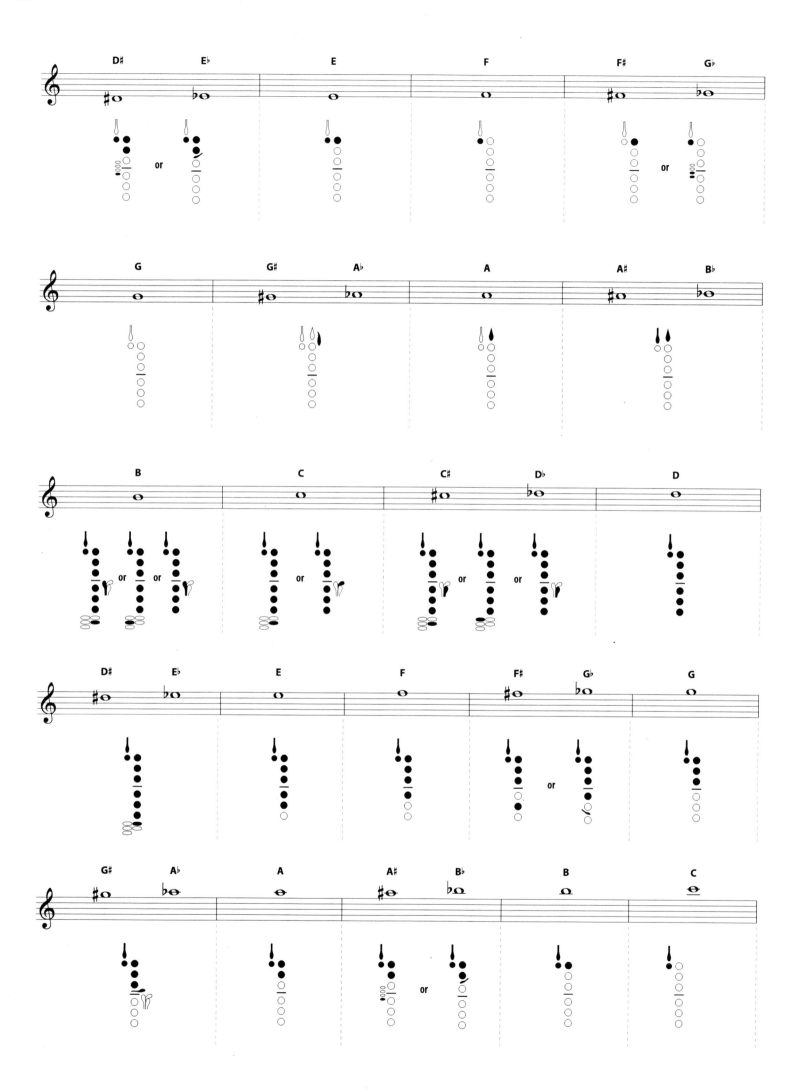